PAUL VS. STATE OF KERALA

VOLUME 2, ISSUE 2 OF BRILLOPEDIA

MRIDULA SHANKER

Copyright © Mridula Shanker
All Rights Reserved.

Contents

Preface

"Start writing, no matter what. The water does not flow until the faucet is turned on".

-Louis L'Amour

Hundreds of students and professors are contributing their work to Brillopedia, we are here to provide ample information about Law and Contemporary issues. Our aim is to provide a platform for today's generation to express their views and ideas on law and contemporary law.

Author

Mridula Shanker

CHAPTER ONE

Abstract

In this paper, the case of **Paul v. State of Kerala** is examined in detail. In the present case the prosecution is the brother of the deceased. He claimed that the appellant had been abusive to her sister physically and mentally ever since their marriage. In contrast, the prosecution claimed that it was a suicide. The learned Principal Sessions Judge held the appellant guilty because it was found that the deceased's death was the direct outcome of blunt force applied on the neck, and also there were other marks on the deceased's body that make it abundantly clear that this is not a case of suicide.

CHAPTER TWO

Facts

- On the 31ˢᵗ of August, 1997, the appellant married Jessy.
- On the tragic day of 11.10.1998, the appellant's mother caused a commotion in their house.
- The deceased, who was depressed, left the house in search of her husband after being subjected to severe harassment, and found him drinking with his friends.
- The appellant attacked his wife in front of his friends.
- Thereafter, on the same night at about 11.00, the appellant throttled her to death.
- Marks of physical violence were present on the body of the deceased.
- The appellant and his mother were charged with cruelty and causing the death of the appellant's wife under Sections 498-A and 302 read with Section 34 of the Indian Penal Code, but were acquitted. Following that, the appellant's mother died.
- However, in a judgment dated March 29, 2012, a Division Bench of the Kerala High Court allowed the State's criminal appeal against the acquittal and set aside the acquittal insofar as it related to the appellant, remanding the case with a direction to dispose of the case by continuing proceedings from the stage of examination under Section 313 Crpc.
- Following the remand, the appellant was found guilty under Section 302 of the IPC by the Principal Sessions Judge,Ernakulum.
- The Appellant was dissatisfied with the judgment and filed an appeal against the principal session judge's decision.

CHAPTER THREE

Issues

   i. Is the fact that the Appellant has been injured sufficient to justify the case being moved from section 302 to section 304 part II of the IPC?

  ii. When does section 304 of IPC applies and whether it is applicable in this case?

 iii. Whether or not the appellant is entitled to get the benefit of exception 4 to section 300 of IPC?

 iv. Whether or not the appellant is entitled to get the benefit of exception 1 to section 300 of IPC?

  v. Did Jessy commit suicide?

CHAPTER FOUR

Contention from both the side

Prosecution

- According to the prosecution, Jessy has been exposed to physical and mental mistreatment in the hands of appellant and his mother since their marriage.
- On the tragic day of 11.10.1998, the appellant's mother made a scene at their house.
- The deceased, who was sad as a result of the harassment, left the house in search of her husband and spotted him drinking with his friends.
- The appellant assaulted his wife in front of his friends.
- The appellant then throttled her to death at 11 p.m. on the same night.

Defence

- A quarrel broke between his mother and his wife.
- He got up early in the morning to urinate, and it was only then, he noticed the deceased hanging from the window railings by a shawl and on his crying PW 2 and 3 came to his room.
- They untied the shawl and the body of Jessy was laid on the bed.
- The appellant's counsel requested that the conviction be changed from section 302 of the IPC to section 304 part II of the IPC, citing the fact that the appellant was also injured.

CHAPTER FIVE

Cases/Authorities Cited

The cases cited were **Pratap Singh vs. State of UP,** Where it was ruled that even if the accused failed to establish his plea, the benefit of the right of private defence cannot reasonably be ruled out from prosecution evidence in a case where the prosecution has not established its case beyond reasonable doubt against the appellant on an essential ingredient of the offence of murder. Also in the case Periasami and Another vs. State of Tamil Nadu, It was established that the law entitles the appellants to the benefit of reasonable doubt. Also the case **State of UP vs. Lakhmi** were referred to where it was ruled that "If an accused admits to any incriminating situation that appears in evidence against him, there is no reason to disregard those confessions just because they were made as part of a defence strategy." Other cases referred to were **Basdev vs. state of Pepsu and State of Andhra Pradesh v. Rayavarapu Punnayya and Another.** The authorities cited in this case were learned principal session judge, "Ernakulum", Division bench of the Kerala High court, K.M. Joseph , Mohan M. Shantanagoudar , Subbarao, J. and Sanjay Kishan Kaul.

CHAPTER SIX

Analysis

- There is a case to be made by the appellant that he was injured. It should be noted that unless the victim is sleeping or unconscious, there will be resistance to throttling. It is not uncommon for the aggressor to sustain injuries. Apart from the neck, other areas of the body were also injured in this case. They denote the aggressor's actions of violence. We are not even asked to comment on whether or not there is anyone else who would be the aggressor in this situation as appellant himself confessed that on the fateful night he and his wife were alone in the bedroom. The appellant, and only the appellant, is responsible for the conduct that resulted in his wife's death.

- Exception I to section 300 of the IPC requires the accused to be deprived of his or her power of control as a result of grave and sudden provocation. In this case, there is no evidence to even faintly imply that the appellant was provoked since, according to the prosecution's argument, the appellant's mother set up a scenario that compelled the deceased to leave the house and look for her husband. There is further talk of the appellant mistreating his wife in front of his friends, and then the appellant throttling her in the middle of the night, this clearly shows that there was a time gap between the provocation and the happening of the event.

- Even exemption 4 to section 300 of the IPC does not apply in this case since there is no evidence to support the finding that a sudden dispute led to a sudden fight based on the appellant's assertion in his written statement that he fell fast asleep.

- It was held by the court in State of **Andhra Pradesh vs. Rayavarapu Punnayya**, that Section 304 of IPC applies only in cases where culpable homicide is not murder, and that if the act amounting to culpable homicide meets any of the four criteria that would bring it under the offence of murder, there would be no reason to allow Section 304 to come into play.

- In this case, section 304 of the IPC cannot be invoked because it is clearly evident that the appellant performed the act that resulted in the death. Given the facts of this case, particularly the injuries sustained, it is apparent that the conduct would fall under the purview of Section 300 of the IPC.

- The death was discovered to be an instantaneous outcome of the blunt force delivered to the deceased's neck. PW1 saw marks of physical assault on the deceased's body. The learned Judge then noted the swelling in the middle of the forehead, as well as an abrasion on the left cheek, which were both mentioned in the inquest report. The dead body's nail clippings and blood samples were collected. The appellant's nail clippings were also taken. Blood in nail clippings, according to the appellant, was caused by an attempt by the dead and the appellant to undo the noose around her neck. However, the court did observe, that PW14's doctor stated that once the ligature was fastened around her neck, the victim would become comatose and unable to move her upper limbs to release it. The Court further observed that according to the written statement provided after remand under 313 Crpc, PW1 and PW3, appellant's brothers, untied the shawl said to have been used by the deceased for committing suicide. This clearly shows thatthe version sought to be introduced in the written statement that there was a fight between his mother and his wife on the date of the incident, during which he was also assaulted by his mother, looks like an embellished version and unacceptable because the incident occurred in the appellant's bedroom, at night, with no other person present. This clearly shows that the appellant is guilty of murder by throttling and that the theory of suicide is unacceptable.

CHAPTER SEVEN

Judgment

The High Court upheld the judgment of the learned Principal Sessions Judge, Ernakulum, who found the appellant guilty under section 302 of the Indian Penal Code (for short "IPC") and sentenced him to life imprisonment and a fine of Rs.10, 000/- because the appellant's actions clearly show that he throttled his wife. None of the exceptions listed in Section 300 are applicable. According to Section 300 of the IPC, the conduct amounts to murder.